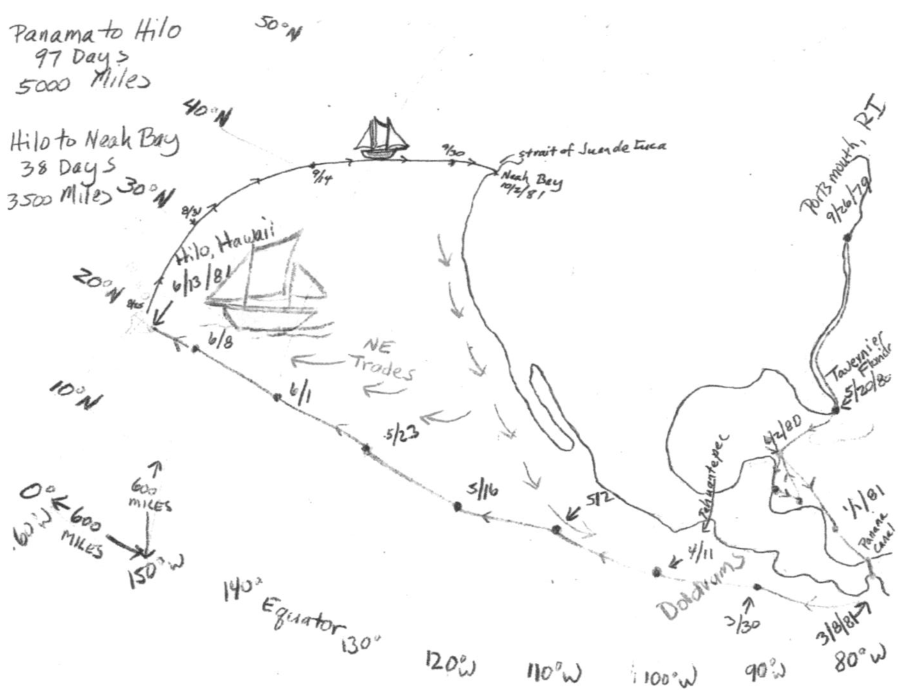
Panama to Hilo
97 Days
5000 Miles
Hilo to Neah Bay
38 Days
3500 Miles
50°N
40°N
30°N
20°N
10°N
0°
Hilo, Hawaii
6/13/81
6/8
6/1
5/23
5/16
5/12
4/11
3/30
3/8/81
NE Trades
Doldrums
8/31
9/14
9/30
strait of Juan de Fuca
Neah Bay
10/2/81
Portsmouth, RI
9/26/79
Tavernier Florida
5/20/80
Tehuantepec
Panama Canal
600 miles
600 MILES
160°W
150°W
140°
Equator
130°
120°W
110°W
100°W
90°W
80°W

Florida
Gulf of Mexico
Key West
Tavernier
5/20/1980
Straits of Florida
Mariel
Havana
Cuba
6/1/90
Isla Mujeres
Yucatan Channel
Wreck of the "Southern Scrap"
Mexico
Belize
Belize City
Isla Utila
Roatan
Guatemala
Honduras
Caribbean Sea
Jamaica
Cabo Gracias a Dios
Nicaragua
Big Corn Island
4/1/1991
Pacific Ocean
Costa Rica
Panama Canal
Panama
3/8/91
Columbia

Companion to
Calypso
Rhyme of the Modern Mariner

Dennis McGuire

Companion to Calypso, Rhyme of the Modern Mariner

The events and conversations in this book have been set down to
the best of the author's ability, although some names and details
have been changed to protect the privacy of individuals.

ISBN 979-8-218-36093-1 (paperback)
ISBN 979-8-218-35969-0 (epub)

First Edition
First Edition: January 2024

www.balladofcalypso.com

TABLE OF CONTENTS

PART I

PART II

Original Preface from the book

Joshua Slocum, along with Howard I. Chapelle and Jack London are the early authors whose work influenced what follows in these pages. Their combined stories, knowledge and real life experience planted the seeds which grew into an insatiable yearning for a sailing adventure.

Slocum's real life account, "Sailing Alone Around the World" entertains the reader from the acquisition of a vessel to the completion of the first round the world, single-handed voyage. An ingenious, determined individual and lifelong creature of the sea, he imparts valuable wisdom in his fascinating tale of the journey.

Howard I. Chapelle's "American Small Sailing Craft" provides the reader with his intimate knowledge of "Traditional Small Sailing Craft, Their Development and Design." One could not help but cultivate an appreciation for the fine lines of the working vessels of years gone by. Their seaworthiness, a product of an evolution in design over several hundred years goes all the way back to old England and beyond.

Jack London's days as an oyster pirate in San Francisco Bay along with his "Voyage of the Snark" add comic relief with many truths embedded, applicable to this day. His story highlights the problems encountered in the building and sailing of a vessel, the results of the project learned in a most rude fashion, far out to sea.

Together with his tales of the inherent, adventurous spirit of the human being, London's stories blur the lines between truth and fiction with an emphasis on hilarity, preceding disastrous consequences. His tragic stories do nothing to discourage the sailor borne to the sea, rather, one is drawn further into its embrace.

Lastly, three authors, and the characters they created must be included with those individuals mentioned above. Joel Chandler Harris, "Br'er Rabbit," Mark Twain, "Huckle berry Finn" and Mort Walker, "Beetle Bailey." Without them in the formative years of this author, in all likelihood this book would not have been written, nor the journey taken.

Dennis McGuire

Preface to the Companion

On completion of the "Ballad of Calypso" I felt compelled to bring out the poetic outline, allowing it to stand alone and relate this adventure to that audience who enjoy the music embedded in rhyming poetry. There are no instruments, however, the foot may begin tapping or the body rocking as the reader follows the story.

As mentioned, this is an outline. It will carry the reader through the entire journey, quickly and smoothly. Where it lacks in prosaic details found in the book, it is filled with the music which the prose interrupts.

Dennis McGuire

PART I

Chapter One
March-September 1979
A JOURNEY BEGINS

Herring Roe on Kelp

Late March in Prince William Sound
icy snow covers the ground
Through glacial waters streaks the spring dawn
great schools of herring have come here to spawn

A circus atmosphere fills the air
as barges're loaded for this grand affair
Kelp buyin' stations these old wooden sleds
an' the place where divers make their beds

Out on the grounds get the skiff ready
air compressor pumpin' steady
Waxin' zippers on the suits
checkin' for holes in bottoms of boots

The condition of the suit top notch throughout
gotta' protect the diver from freezin' out
Air hose coiled, kelp boxes stacked
with charcoal 'n cotton the air filter's packed

There's a new beauty down below
across the undersea landscape
a fresh herring spawn snow
The next generation springin' to life here
on ribbon, hair 'n elephant ear

Clams, urchins 'n cucumbers're fine
but herring roe kelp divin's really sublime
Swimmin' straight down into this
icy cold brine
fillin' our skiff with a product devine

Divin' hard eight days in a row
we have eight grand to show
for that sailboat we'd been a wishin'
long before we started fishin'

The quality this season does entice
a very satisfying healthy price
Leavin' the grounds far astern
headed to town with money to burn!

Finding Calypso

Rode the "Empire Builder" to the eastern seaboard
beat the docks for boats our funds could afford
Lookin' aroun' an' whaddaya know
wound up at the Newport Used Boat Show!

Hop a fence middle of the night
'cause we spot a boat that looks just right
When mornin' comes an' the show's open
Calypso will be ours we're a hopin'

Built by shipwright A.A. Bernard
nineteen fifty two in his backyard
A sturdy little ketch of twenty six feet
this boat deal's hard to beat

Inside ballast makes her stable
we slap all our money on the table
Then Marie with tears in her eyes
to her little boat she says her goodbyes

Portsmouth

The Stone Bridge Marina in Portsmouth we stay
start divin' for quahogs other side of the quay
Every day I go a clammin'
on Calypso Pat's a jammin'

Loadin' the dinghy with cherrystones
workin' fingers to the bones
Scratchin' out a hundred bucks a day
from the bottom of Narragansett Bay

Out of a woodpile appears a kitty
name him "Woody" 'cause it's kinda witty
Woody completes our crew of three
an' soon we'll be sailin' cross the sea

Block Island Sound

Doesn't take long workin' on her steady
Calypso's gone through 'n made ready
An' when the moon's just a sliver
Calypso's sailin' down the Sakonnet River

The voyage doesn't start out just right
nearly hit rocks very first night
Sailin' 'n bailin' I gotta say
Calypso's leakin' thirty gallons today

Block Island Sound 's
our sea trial grounds
Where squally weather has plenty of fetch
we discover the nuances of sailin'
a gaff rigged ketch

Raise the mizzen 'n sheet 'er tight
Calypso holds in irons just right
Hoist the mainsail, throat an' peak together
while Calypso bobs obediently to weather

Backwind the mizzen, mainsail bellies out
raise the jib an' come about
Whooshin' 'n gurglin' a soothing sound
for the tropics, Calypso's bound

Eighty gallons pumped this day
while Calypso's makin' excellent way
By the time we get to be good sailors
looks like we're gonna be real good bailers

Port Jefferson

At Port Jefferson we haul her out
to see what this leakin's all about
There's small geysers squirtin'
our poor little boat's really hurtin'

Water's shootin' from her garboard
corked her tight port 'n starboard
Local folks helped in every way
till Calypso slides back into the Bay

New York City

Distant thunder can be heard rollin'
New York City bells're tollin'
Long Island Sound this windless night
there's skyscrapers comin' into sight

Approachin' Hell Gate the fair wind dies
engine starts, sputters an' sighs
Crankin' on that "BlueJacket Twin"
got bloody knuckles agin'!

Jump to the halyards 'n raise full sail
broke down now with an engine fail
Under Hell Gate Bridge caught in whirlpools
Calypso's lookin' like a ship o' fools!

Helicopter takin' off on her right
blows poor Calypso right outa sight
At this point I could give a hill 'a beans
Calypso crashes in Jamaica Queens!

We need a battery so go ashore
found a gas station 'n the fella says "Shore!
jess' gimme fifty bucks 'n have a cigar"
then he goes 'n rips off somebody's car!

Makin' our way through New York City
sailin' right by the Statue o' Liberty
Sailin' through that thunderous roar
Calypso's course set for the New Jersey shore

Chapter Two
Fall -Winter 1979
INTRACOASTAL WATERWAY

Sailin' 'n bailin' I gotta say
Calypso's makin' fifty miles a day
Into Atlantic City we scoot
do some gamblin' 'n make some loot

Boardwalk 'n Park Place don't treat the crew well
left Atlantic City no money 'n nothin' left to sell
Blew our shot at gettin' rich
back to sailin' this muddy little ditch

"Muddy little ditch you say?
this is the Intracoastal Waterway"
An engineering marvel tucked away from the sea
Calypso sails in peace and tranquility

Caught a fresh breeze up the Delaware River
November winds givin' us a shiver
In the C 'n D canal shelter's found
alas, lotta commercial traffic runnin' around

Tugs 'n barges big 'n strong
Chuggin' by all night long
through the darkness they pull their load
Rockin' 'n rollin' our tiny abode

Chesapeake Bay

Autumn colors fill Chesapeake Bay
as Calypso sails along her way
Back n' forth into the wind we tack
find another cove, anchor 'n kick back

Crossin' the Potomac at night's a fright
Calypso put up one hell of a fight
River and wind throws everything at her
till she safely drops anchor in the Wicomico Spider

Great Dismal Swamp

In the Dismal Swamp
Calypso's engine breaks down
'bout the same time we run her hard agroun'
"Rinky Dink" to the rescue now
kedgin' anchor off the starboard bow

Grunt 'n groan, pull with all ya got
gotta' get Calypso offa' this shallow spot
With every purchase ya' take another bight
Calypso moves ever so slight

Off the bottom she finally goes a bumpin'
an' we get that ol' motor a thumpin'
Drop anchor 'n get some rest
for tomorrow may be another test

North Carolina

Anchors aweigh on this frozen dawn
through swamps 'n byways Calypso glides along
Layin' her wake on a mirrored pond
sailin' in silence with grace of a swan

Albemarle winds chill the air from the north
Calypso continues to sally forth
The Alligator-Pungo has stories to tell
of the Underground Railroad
'n people runnin' from Hell
Calypso glides quietly on these waters of mystery
cypress standin' silent witness history

Sail On

Inside Cape Hatteras 'n the Outer Banks
give that ol' motor fifty cranks
Cursin' 'n cajolin' to no avail
Pamlico Sound sees Calypso set sail

An' sail she does with so much heart
Calypso's happy that ol' engine won't start!
For she's a sailor true as can be
a hardy little vessel 'n her crew of three

Gettin' right down to the nitty gritty
Calypso sails into Morehead City
Make repairs on that Blue Jacket Twin
Calypso's up 'n runnin' agin'!

Near the bed keep a potato handy
for a bilge alarm it's a dandy
Toss the spud 'n hear a splash
for the bilge pump you must dash

Pumpin' the bilge a daily chore
this ol' girl's leakin' more 'n more
'Bout the time ya can't take the stress
Calypso starts leakin' less 'n less

Over a thousand miles she's motored 'n sailed
an' as many gallons we certainly have bailed
Through the Carolinas sailin's sublime
runnin' wing 'n wing cross the Georgia state line

St. Simon's Island

We're catchin' onto this sailin' life very well
an' find ourselves yearnin' for the oceans' swell
One more bridge we have to pass
then for the ocean Calypso will dash

Many bridges 'n locks negotiated along the way
but the tide's ebbin' hard in Frederica River today
Start crankin' on that Blue Jacket Twin
got bloody knuckles 'n broke down agin'!

Bridge is closed blockin' her way
total destruction now just yards away
Hoist sails, crank the helm harda' port
'cross the river lay St. Simons resort

Caught in the grip of a mighty stream
winds' comin' down river abaft her beam
Across this river lies a dock
where a number of folks have begun to flock

Close hauled on the last tack
fightin' ebb tide 'n bridge back to back
When Calypso makes her final turn
the Saint Simons Bridge's right off her stern

Plenty of handshakes 'n hugs all around
people're happy we're safe 'n sound
This scene has played out before
while folks watched standin' helpless on shore

On St. Simons Island we find respite
celebratin' late into New Year's night
Islanders help out the followin' day
eager to lend a hand in every way

Repairin' the Blue Jacket 'n haulin' provisions
helpin' with navigation decisions
When St. Simons Bridge opens at six o'clock
Calypso lets go her lines from the dock

The Gulf Stream

A strong ebb tide pullin' her free
Calypso's bow tastes the salt of the sea
Icy bowsprit sparklin' in sunlight
a twenty knot nor'wester with its freezin' bite

Out the inlet 'n down to its mouth
Calypso stands to the south
A few hours sailin' under jib 'n mizzen
the crew's pleased with their decision

An invisible warm wall Calypso sails through
under her bow the ocean turns blue
Sargasso seaweed floats abeam
Calypso sails the mighty Gulf Stream

Phosphorescence streamin'
off dolphins leapin'
Calypso 'n crew watch with glee
acrobats on this moonlit sea

Night Raid

A ship's lights appear late in the night
then a Coast Guard Cutter comes within sight
Calypso's boarded 'n searched bow to stern
while the crew's tempers begin a slow burn

Let those sheets 'n halyards drop
lay in the trough 'n let Calypso flop
Cross the deck that main boom comes a sweepin'
duckin' for cover these Coasties're a leapin'

Back to their boat they scatter for safety
their retreat very hasty
Didn't know Calypso's sails lay a flappin'
on account of an angry Capn'!

UFO

The followin' night there's a strange sight
off to the west appears an odd light
Darted left, darted right
then stood still shinin' bright

Space travelers seem quite curious to know
'bout little Calypso bobbin' below
The light disappears without a sound
for outer space they are bound

Ponce De Leon Inlet

Two days more
sailin' the Florida shore
Cape Canaveral off the starboard bow
turn for land an' the Intra-Coastal now

Ponce de Leon inlet with the flood tide
the rules of the road a boat must abide Chapter
Traffic can be heavy 'n hairy at times
Calypso's a sailin' 'n tackin' on dimes

Chapter 3
Winter-Spring 1980
FLORIDA

Florida Keys lay just ahead
pockets're empty gotta' make some bread
A few more inlets 'n bridges to pass
maybe get some dough 'n buy some gas

Key Largo

Key Largo's close at hand
Calypso drops anchor in white sand
Ballyhoo seinin's what we chose
to cure those money woes

Miniature swordfish complete with a snout
'round colorful corals small schools swim about
Hand pullin' purse seine makes the back sore
'cause these folks don't know
that's what hydraulics're for!

Tavernier

Since divin' is my forte'
I embark on a salvage divin' sortie
Raise a boat to get some cash
but the owner he tries to dash

He sneaks out from behind a trailer
an' with a crowbar whacks this sailor
I take his weapon 'n throw it willy nilly
then commence to slap this coward silly

The cops, they arrive on scene
an' of course they intervene
Agin' for money we've come up short
lookin' for work we abort

The Last Straw

To rent the Rinky Dink we get an offer
a hundred bucks goes into the coffer
It's a few days later when we know
never again the Rinky Dink we'll row

Another failed attempt to raise money
I say "let's sell the engine Honey!"
We say good-bye to the "Blue-Jacket Twin"
Calypso sails on, no more bloody knuckles agin'

Chapter 4
March-September 1979
CUBA

Mariel Boat Lift

Set sail for Cuba we're gonna make a lotta' hay
the "Mariel Boatlift's" underway!
By the way did I forget to say?
Calypso's still leakin' thirty gallons a day!

A thousand bucks for every soul we put aboard
we'll come back to Florida with a whole horde!
Unfortunately it does not happen
becalmed with sails loosely flappin'

Cuban Fishing Boat

Out front of Havana on this windless day
a fishin' boat comes steamin' our way
Side by side, rafted together
fishermen all we're birds of a feather

Cuban Gun Boat

Just havin' lunch 'n to our dismay
there's a Cuban gunboat comin' outa' the bay
Our fishermen friends must say goodbye
no time for mango pie

Big grey warship headin' our way
passin' too close 'n tears off a stay
Driftin' on that starboard tack
Calypso gets sideswiped with a whack

They swing back 'round 'n throw us a line
But they do not ask if we'd like to dine
Cigar smokin' sailors line the rail
Starin' down at this little boat under sail

We tell 'em "we're Alaska bound!"
The Captain thinks our minds unsound!
"We're kickin' crazy people outa' Cuba today
an' you are not invited to stay!"

Calypso's let go on a lee shore
clawin' her way off as so many times before
With the streets of Havana in plain view
Calypso sets her course anew

I-Ching Navigation

Three coins and a book appear
for makin' a decision on which way to steer
What the crew shall now do here
the I-Ching makes quite clear

For Mexico we'll now sail!
an' with that we continue to bail
Cause the water's still comin' in
an' if we stop it'll surely win!

Celestial Navigation

Off to the west Mexico lay
nearly three hundred nautical miles away
No longer sailin' with a map's details
an empty chart Calypso now sails

Pat learns quickly what it's all about
when those celestial navigation tools're brought out
Sextant measures angles to the sun, moon 'n stars
soon we're friends with Aldebaran 'n Mars

The radio bongs time, angles're measured
then turn to the books so treasured
Sight reduction tables n' almanac
keep Calypso 'n crew on the right tack

Among constellations Calypso travels
when navigation's mysteries Pat unravels
An empty blue Gulf at first hint of light
the crew of Calypso takes the morning sight

Big Weather

Even when weather is calm 'n fair
storms appear out of thin air
Cumulonimbus risin' thousands of feet in the sky
hard wind 'n lightning bolts as the storms pass by

Race to the halyards 'n drop sail
tie the jib off at the rail
Lash everythin' on deck real good
with Mr. Nimbus in the neighborhood

Dodgin' big ships always a fright
passin' Calypso in the dark of night
Addin' to a fear we begin to dread
the Yucatan Strait lay dead ahead

A hundred miles wide, ten thousand feet deep
fifty foot mountains rollin' 'n steep
Calypso sails with a sassy sashay
all the way to Cabo Catoche

Enterin' our second week at sea
a gruelin' test of endurance this sail has come to be
Twenty-four sevens at the helm
exhaustion threatens to overwhelm

Chapter 5
Summer 1980
MEXICO

First sight of land we make course corrections
according to navigation charts 'n Sailin' Directions
"A low lyin' bare sand spit"
proclaims the Directions ditty
instead there rises Cancun city!

After recoverin' from the shock
we know Cancun city we'll not dock
"Where to now?" We ask
"At Isla Mujeres our anchor we'll cast!"

Just off the coast this tiny island lay
twenty nautical miles away
A bone in her teeth 'n leavin' a frothy trail
the northeast trades fill Calypso's mainsail

Drop anchor back of the bay
next to where fishin' boats stay
After fourteen days 'n five hundred miles
Calypso 'n crew're wearin' broad smiles

Snorklin' 'n fishin's how our days're spent
no worries on how we'll pay the rent
A kilo of tortillas for a few pesos
a few more centavos 'n we're eatin' huevos

Southern Scrap

There comes a stormy day
when a fellow sailor sails into the bay
Chock-a-block loaded to the gunnels with crap
a little yellow life boat the "Southern Scrap"

The Southern Scrap of steel she's built
her patchwork sails a psychedelic quilt
A lively fellow Cosmic Kris
bouncin' aroun' in a never endin' state of bliss

Televisions, radios, mix masters 'n clocks
shoppin' carts, toilet seats, hub caps 'n socks
A boatload of prime American trash
Cosmic Kris's gonna turn into cash

Mexican Fishermen

Those Mexican fishermen on the beach
a lesson this sailor they intend to teach
There's a great spot for Conch divin' they know
an' their superior skills they're determined to show

They don mask snorkel 'n fins
their confidence displayed in wide grins
Sixty feet deep where Calypso's anchor dropped
into the water my fishermen friends popped

This sailor has a mask
but without fins 'n snorkel
he has a very difficult task
Snorkels 'n fins great advantage they made
but this sailors' secret, he's a diver by trade

Their competition does not end there
now, who could provide the tastiest fare?
Every day we're invited to dinner
on a different boat determined to be the winner!

These seventy foot trawlers have freezers below
crammed with the catch from their daily tow
Swordfish 'n snapper come up from the hold
An' every night a new feast would unfold!

Snowy Egret

Followin' the day of the local fiesta
crew 'n cat're startled from their siesta
A snowy egret flutters in through the hatch
an' for Woody the boatcat an easy catch

On the cabin sole this bird alights
an' Woody's got it in his sights
In an instant that Yankee cat's there
givin' this poor bird a lethal stare

With Woody's nose inches away
the bird closes its eyes an' begins to sway
This catbird situation's tense
the crew's watchin' in great suspense

Woody kept cockroaches off the boat
chased away birds wantin' to rest an' float
Now the crew's seein' somethin' strange occurin'
'cause Woody the Yankee cat's a purrin'!?

On one leg, snowy egret's standin' there
the other leg's tucked away somewhere
The little bird's head cocks to one side
the snowy egret stood there an' died

Of what might have occurred the crew's certain
but somehow, Woody knew this bird's hurtin'
Cause a purrin' cat with no tail twitchin'
for a fight its not itchin'

How Woody was aware
even a guess we would not dare
But somethin' else the crew's not understandin'
how a bird could die an' on one leg still be standin'?!

Yucatan Barrier Reef

With hurricane season arrivin' soon
Calypso sets sail under a waxin' moon
Fillin' her sails with a fresh northeast breeze
bowsprit pointin' straight at Belize

The ruins of Tulum
through jungle growth they're peekin'
Of course Calypso she just continues leakin'
Along this jagged reef we make our way
still pumpin' thirty gallons a day

Wreck of the Southern Scrap

For Southern Scrap's well being we have our fears
'cause Cosmic Kris has light years 'tween the ears
Far off in the distance one can just make it out
is the wreck of the Southern Scrap
there's no doubt

Televisions, radios, mix masters 'n clocks,
shopping carts, toilet seats, hub caps 'n socks,
Pots 'n pans, dish drainers 'n bleach,
looks like "Saint Vinnies" crashed on the beach!

Shards of twisted metal
a hank of psychedelic sail it seems
is all that remains of the Southern Scrap
'n Cosmic Kris's sailin' dream

Calypso 'n crew can only sail on
along this rugged coast
An' to Cosmic Kris 'n Southern Scrap
we raise our farewell toast

Risky Passage

A break in the reef points the way
from these rollin' blue seas to a quiet bay
Helm hard over sheet'er down tight
gotta' hit that clear spot exactly right

Gnarly white water crashin' close by
Calypso makes her perilous try
Three feet of draft is all she carries
but on that reef her bow she buries!

Of becomin' a shipwreck
the crew has good reason to dread
With visions of Southern Scrap fresh in the head
The wind 'n surge push our little craft
an' we heel Calypso over so she'll carry less draft

Calm water beckons
destruction threatens
'Cross the barrier reef Calypso crashes her way
into the open arms of Ascencion Bay

Bahia de la Ascension

A surprise awaits Calypso
when she drops anchor at Vigio Chico
A wizened old man in a village of empty huts
an' beaches covered with coconuts!

Setting to work the crew wastes no time
loadin' little Calypso right to the waterline
A boatload of coconuts has the crew giddy
when Calypso sails into Belize City

Chapter 6
Summer 1980
BELIZE CUSTOMS

Havin' just arrived from 'ol Mexico
Mr. Customs Man sneers "you have coco!"
To which we reply with great sincerity"
We've loaded our boat for free!"

Mr. Customs Man appears irritated at our glee
an' becomes very angry with me!
"We have about a ton to be realistic"
an' with that Mr. Customs' man goes ballistic!

This poor sailor can no longer endure
intimidation from Mr. Officer
"Come to Calypso 'n see for yourself"
an' behold!
A load of coconuts top shelf!

Calypso's coco comes from palm tree
it's very plain to see
At the root of this hubbub?
Mr. Customs Man's coco
comes from a shrub!

"Wooden sailin' vessels in Belize abound
are there any boatyards around?
Poor Calypso's leakin' in a bad way
an' we're pumpin' a hundred gallons a day"

Mr. Customs' man fell back 'n laughed
pointin' at our little vessel "you must be daft!
Sailin' to Alaska in a sinkin' boat?
go see Jones he'll keep you afloat!"

Intimidation's set aside now
Calypso 'n crew receive a welcomin' bow
with this nutty issue resolved
The conversation now evolved

"Through that bridge 'n take a couple jogs
the yard's on your portside the one with all the dogs!"
Up Haulover Creek we make our deal with Jones
in his yard full of boats' n their broken bones

Jones's Boatyard

A turnstile haulout with locals lendin' a hand
cranks Calypso from the water onto dry land
Lead shipwright's "Poppy" an' he goes after the rot
has a crew rippin' 'n tearin' on the spot

Away with the bulwarks reef out the seams
scrapin' 'n paintin' this boat of our dreams
Two thousand miles has poor Calypso ailin'
but when Poppy's done we're no longer bailin'!

New Life for Woody

On what goes through a cat's mind
this sailor would have normally not opined
But when Calypso cut loose from the dock
we suffer a bit of a shock

Sailing Belize

With Calypso rebuilt 'n no water comin' in
the next leg of this journey can now begin
A great opportunity to give her new sail a try
we let that number one genny fly!

The Trade Winds belly that big sail out
an' Calypso now proves she's very stout
This oversize cotton balloon we've had built
carries Calypso full tilt!

We say goodbye to the city of Belize
Calypso's sails fill with a freshenin' breeze
On the outer cays we spend our days
explorin', snorkelin' 'n anchorin' in small bays

Live Boating

With shallow water 'n light winds prevailin'
I'd do a little scoutin' while Pat does the sailin'
Clingin' to the tow rope watchin' coral heads pass by
a purple sail catches the eye

Then another 'n a 'nother 'n a 'nother
an'a 'nother 'n a 'nother an' O' brother!
Now there's a thousand or more
the sails of the Portugese-Man-O-War!

Tentacles hangin' down 'n stingin'
this poor sailor starts a singin'
Stop the boat m'dear
an' get me outa' here!

Chapter 7
September 1980
HONDURAS

The Islands of Honduras're soon off our bow
an' navigation becomes very exactin' now
Straight ahead a nest of coral reefs lay
directly in the path to Turtle Bay

Isla Utila

Strong winds push Calypso along
when it becomes clear she's gone very wrong!
Escape to seaward's blocked by a reef
any moment now Calypso'll come to grief

Shorten sail to jib 'n mizzen
to deal with this danger which has arisen
Jump to the bowsprit lead line in hand
gotta' keep Calypso over bare patches of sand

Trapped

For the bottom keepin' a steady gaze
workin' the boat through this deadly maze
Into the lee of Isla Utila Calypso threads her way
findin' herself trapped in a dead end bay

Several days're spent snorkelin' about
but alas for Calypso there's no way out
A cayuka from the island now comes into sight
these friendly Islanders're aware of our plight

A tow through the maze 'n shallows we received
an' for this local knowledge we're much relieved
Soon we have our anchor down
right out front of Utila town

"Bucket of Blood"

The "Bucket of Blood's" the local hang out
reggae 'n beer's what it's all about
The place gets packed 'n folks start dancin'
From under the Wurlitzer
coconut crabs come a'prancin'!

Hurricane Hermine

Over the shortwave radio
comes scary news for Calypso
Destructive wind bearin' down today
an' Isla Utila's standin' right in the way

The Islanders have great concern
for Calypso has nowhere to turn
Hurricane Hermine's comin' her way
an' she's anchored in an open roadstead bay

Again local knowledge plays a major role
an' from another cayuka Calypso welcomes a tow
Deep into the mangrove swamp she's tucked away
safe from the monster approachin' Turtle Bay

Lashed Calypso to the mangroves
from every direction
The villagers said
"this'll give you the best protection!"
With limbs 'n roots we toiled 'n wrestled
now in the arms of Utila we're nestled

Calypso 'n crew're left alone
the world grows dark twisted limbs groan
The wind pipes up to hurricane force
Calypso bucks like a rodeo horse

Throughout the night Hermine vents her wrath
bent on destroyin' everythin' in her path
Torrents of rain poundin' down
will anythin' be left of Utila town?

The mornin' dawn's quiet when villagers return
all 're safe we're relieved to learn
Mud in the streets 'n store signs down
Utila's certainly one hardy little town

Passage to Roatan

With the passin' of Hermine
hard wind 'n rain have ceased
Calypso says goodbye to Utila
an' sails fair winds east
current 'n breeze workin' in her favor
conditions sailors really savor

Within an hour
weather turns sour
Ten foot seas breakin' heavy
Calypso shortens sail her course held steady

Into the seas crashin' 'n tumblin' all day
to Roatan Island just twenty miles away
A halyard gets loose 'n starts a whippin'
then lets go high in the riggin'

Goin' aloft with a fresh halyard
Calypso's gallopin' like a horse for the barnyard
Climbin' the mizzen in a wild sea
swingin' in the riggin' like a chimpanzee!

Back on deck lines squared away
losin' our light it's the end of the day
Reef strewn Roatan now in sight
blowin' forty five 'n turnin' to night

With this treacherous scene so near
now to our horror we cannot steer!
The helm's just spinnin' free
Calypso's rudderless in a heavy sea

Caught in the throes of a full gale's fury
gotta make repairs in a hurry
Wind 'n sea're ragin'
Calypso's steerin' gears' they ain't engagin'

Hove to as darkness envelops
a grave situation now develops
Less than a mile to a reef
where Calypso'll surely come to grief

Grabbin' bailin' wire 'n twine
this is the moment mariners shine
Tearin' into the problem at hand
for this could be Calypso's last stand

A good repair makes her safe
Calypso's no longer a rudderless waif
Jib 'n mizzen sheeted tight
helm in hand she's back in the fight

Drop the mizzen 'n come about
this sail to Roatan's a rout
A reef in the jib, weather on her stern
Calypso rides easy after the turn

Standin' off Utila at the break of day
Roatan Island's thirty miles away
Over twenty four hours since we started
Calypso's just a mile from where she departed!

Our boat's proven she's very stout
"we'll make Roatan without a doubt!"
Up with the genny, mizzen 'n main
spirits're soarin' 'n feelin' a touch insane!

Calypso drives hard against the breeze
boundin' along in choppy seas
Just before nightfall the wind becomes fickle
Calypso finds herself in another pickle

Gnarly white teeth abound
there's danger all around
By jagged corals Calypso's surrounded
an' in grave danger of bein' grounded!

Sailin's now extremely tricky
this situation's very sticky
Under jib 'n mizzen through this maze we're tackin'
lead line 'n a star keep Calypso safely trackin'

Into Coxen Hole, Calypso winds her way
splash of the anchor signals end of the day
Restin' in an anchorage so hard fought
the peace 'n quiet Calypso had sought

Havin' dropped anchor durin' the night
Calypso's crew wakes to another fright!
The local boneyard's across the beach, off our stern
an' in the morn' when we pull the pick
the wicked truth we learn

Durin' the night while logs we're sawin'
On our anchor line the coral reef was gnawin'
The rode held together by a single thread
nearly lost Calypso where Islanders bury their dead!

In Roatan we choose to rest
exhausted from this most recent test
forty eight hours for a thirty mile run
relaxin' now under a tropical sun

The Big Picture

Reassessin' our current position
time has come for a strategic decision
Headwinds 'n dangers lay ahead like a beast
Cabo Gracias a Dios lies two hundred fifty miles east

In light of situation with which we're dealin'
we find Isla Mujeres, very appealin'
Three hundred miles north by northwest
this is the tack that'll serve us best

The way to Panama's 'round the Cape
an' from its treachery Calypso must escape
From Isla Mujeres we'll make our tack
at Cabo Gracias we'll have another crack!

Northeast trades settled 'n steady
Calypso's shipshape 'n ready
Cast off lines 'n wave goodbye
let the jib 'n mizzen fly!

Chapter 8
ISLA MUJERES

Wind's twenty five knots 'n gustin'
through gnarly blue seas Calypso's bustin'
On a close reach sheets hauled tight
Honduras disappears in the fadin' light

Three days we sail this fresh breeze
playfully boundin' through Caribbean seas
Approachin' Cozumel on the third night
we suffer yet another fright!

To a light ahead Calypso makes her way
"Cozumel Island" charts 'n compass say
Slack the sheets 'n put the wind abeam
all's well it certainly does seem

Without warnin' comes an unwelcome surprise
when gnashin' jaws of ocean arise
Calypso's sailin' straight into the teeth
of the great Yucatan Barrier Reef!

Put down the helm let the jib 'n main go slack
come about sharply on the port tack
Our compass appears to be in error
an' thus the source of this new terror

A magnetic disturbance is very strong
causin' our trusty compass to go way wrong
Calypso nearly meets her doom
in front of the ruins of Tulum!

This ancient reef is strewn with bones
an' remains of galleons' ballast stones
Of these dangers Calypso sails clear
the poundin' reef she can no longer hear

Only eighty miles left for this trek
so lucky not to be just another wreck
A northerly current, an easterly breeze
these last miles're covered with ease

At Isla Mujeres Calypso hauls tourists for cheap
with snorklers 'n sunbathers she earns her keep
Makin' a few pesos 'n divin' for fun
easy livin' under a tropical sun

Yucatan Treasure

Golden George comes on the scene
to find the "Atocha" is his dream
Long blonde hair, jewels 'n gold
George's lookin' big 'n bold

Searchin' for galleons more than just a pleasure
his catamaran's loaded with Spanish treasure
Bein' a diver the temptation's strong
an' half hopin' he'd take me along

Chapter 9
December 1980

CABO GRACIAS A DIOS

On Pat's return it's time to regroup
Doug comes aboard, now we're a troupe!
Calypso returns to the Caribbean Sea
with her happy go lucky crew of three!

Settin' off on a glorious broad reach
takin' turns at the helm three hours each
Lookin' at the chart it does appear
Panama's 'bout a thousand miles from here

For two days, sailin's a thrill
until dark clouds the skies they fill
White caps slappin' 'n splashin' the hull
announcin' sailin' won't be dull

The intensity of the wind havin' risen
Calypso heaves to under reefed mizzen
In Calypso's ability, we have no doubt
nuthin' to do but ride this one out

Once the storm abates star sights're taken
on course to the Cape there's no mistaken'
A hundred more miles or so
round Cabo Gracias a Dios we'll go

On Pat's navigational skills we rely
when she appears at the hatch she's not shy
She's bundled the Sun Moon 'n Arcturus
with father time in order to assure us

"We'll see palm trees in one hour" is her claim
The doubters checkin' watches make it a game
She has our position down exactly
an' announces it so matter-of-factly

As the sixty minute mark nears
our navigator may be incorrect it appears
An' when that sixty minute mark has passed
nuthin' but empty blue ocean so vast

Just thirty seconds more pass by
somethin' on the horizon catches the eye
There's palm trees straight off our bowsprit!
Our navigator has just nailed it!

New Year 1981

At Man-o-War Caye a New Year's toast
Calypso stands off the Nicaraguan Coast
On Great Corn a quiet bay beckons
our next anchorage the crew reckons

Genny 'flyin' in a twenty five knot breeze
surfin' down these blue mountain seas
Strong northeast trades broad reach sailin's grand
two hundred more miles we'll drop anchor in sand

Chapter 10
January 1981
NICARAGUA

Great Corn Island

The trades now veerin' to a close reach
Calypso claws her way toward Brig Bay Beach
Tedious tackin' full sail flyin'
then the wind, it just starts dyin'

Wind's quit. Calypso's driftin' outa the bay
then lo! There's a Cuban gunboat comin' our way
Wonderful hospitality they immediately show
tossin' a line an' givin' Calypso a tow

Sandinista Commandant

The Cuban crew's all smokin' cigars
'n wearin' shorts
A mustachioed Commandant
receives our passports
"Welcome to Corn Island" is his decree
then commences to give us the third degree!

"Goin' to Alaska in that little boat?!"
then makes like he's shiverin'
'n puttin' on a coat!
Folks roar with laughter as the Commandant teased
it's obvious with Calypso's arrival he's very pleased

Of this island he's extremely proud
an' as he speaks there gathers a crowd
When the Commandant ends his welcomin' speech
a wonderful soccer game erupts on the beach!

With the game havin' played itself out
the Commandant takes the crew out 'n about
This military gentleman now our guide
we're shown the source of his great pride

For Nicaragua these're tumultuous times
Somozas' regime overthrown for its many crimes
The Sandinista Liberation Front now looms large
of this fledgling government they're now in charge

Over the Corn Islands the Commandant presided
pointin' out the mansion where Somoza had resided
An' during those war torn days
he'd personally set Somoza's home ablaze

A Teacher for the Island

Pat's a teacher the Commandant discovers
an' his idea he soon uncovers
A house 'n food will be provided
so the Island will have a teacher if she so decided

On the surface a fortuitous event
until our new found friends begin to vent
The Islanders express their great frustration
our food 'n shelter's inadequate compensation

When folks hear
no cash their teacher will be earning
The crew witness an anger deeply burning
"We're not communists you see,
Cubans're here takin' our jobs 'n workin' for free!"

Of the open wounds of war the crew's now aware
an' it certainly gives them a darn good scare
The people're ready to do battle
the crew decides, "We better skedaddle!"

Generosity

We inform our friends it's time to go
an' extreme generosity they now show
"Follow the boy on the donkey" they said
an' through lush jungle Calypso's crew is led

The donkey's loaded right up to his ears
so much food brings the crew to tears
For Panama Calypso now sets her sails
fruits 'n vegetables lashed to the rails!

Pearly white clouds racin' up high
Calypso's locomotive in a light blue sky
Ridin' a wave train with a chop on top
The Isthmus of Panama Calypso's next stop

A sliver of land sixty miles wide
a great ocean hidin' on the other side
Three hundred miles south
there's a path cut straight
to where adventure lies in wait

Chapter 11
January 1981
PANAMA

Colon Yacht Club

The Colon Yacht Club welcomes the invasion
of vessels 'n travelers of every persuasion
Two continents 'n two oceans intersect here
the crew ties up an' enjoy a cold beer

A beehive of activity on the dock
crews makin' preparations 'round the clock
World cruisers from afar
cuttin' deals in the Yacht Club bar

Self-Steering Windvane

Trade off the air compressor
for a wind vane we name Hector
Doug refashions Hector makin' it ready
assurin' Calypso's course will hold steady

Super Hydra

At the end of the dock there's a mutiny
the crew has their cap'n under great scrutiny
Super Hydra's taken over by the crew
an' Doug jumps into the middle of that stew

As captain's bodyguard Doug's now hired
by this capn' who'd just been fired
An' while this's all goin' down
Calypso's lookin' for a tow outa' town

La Cucaracha

Our Swedish neighbors have a mutiny
of a different sort
an' their journey they're nearly ready to abort
A gazillion cockroaches've taken command
so bold they look ya in the eye 'n take a stand!
On cabin walls tables 'n floors, insects scurry
runnin' aroun' in a great big hurry
An' when ya catch 'em eatin' yer lunch
whack 'em good 'n they go crunch!

Sea Horse

A boat outa Norway catches Doug's eye
price is right 'n he makes a great buy
Holdin' now the reins of his "Sea Horse"
together they'll chart a brand new course

Transit Preparations

Food 'n necessities stored
a hundred twenty gallons of water aboard
Only one thing Calypso's missin'
the putt putt putt of her 'ol engine

Intrepid

For a vessel with power
the docks we scour
A fishin' vessel transitin' the Canal
the "Intrepid's" happy to be Calypso's new pal
This connection's really terrific
'cause Calypso's gettin' a tow
all the way to the Pacific!

The Big Ditch

Whirlpools 'n upwellins' as the locks fill
slimy green walls give the crew a chill
Steel gates closin' screech 'n moan
Calypso's lines take the strain 'n groan

Locked in an elevator where water rages
Calypso rises eighty five feet in three stages
Rafted snug to her escort it's very soon
when Calypso enters Lake Gatun

Cross the lake the two boats race
Intrepid's towin' Calypso at a furious pace
At Pedro Miguel Calypso's on a hillside
a great ocean awaits at the end of this ride

Of the journey ahead the crew's thoughts're mixed
of the wide expanse before them
they stand transfixed
This bundle of wood 'n nails
driven by wind 'n sails
out in the Pacific Ocean with big ships 'n whales

PART II

Chapter 12
March 1980
PACIFIC OCEAN

Final preparations for the voyage ahead
makin' sure unwanted critters're dead
Soakin' banana stalks over the side
eliminatin' tarantulas without insecticide

Smugglers Cove

One last problem needs solvin'
for finances're fast dissolvin'
At the yacht club a nefarious scheme
had been planned
Now the remedy to our financial woes
is close at hand

Calypso sails into a secret bight
just before the cover of night
A cayuka paddles out from shore
to see what offer we have in store

A hundred dollars is the end of our cash
an' for this we hope to acquire a small stash
The locals want a forty horse outboard
an' for that they'll put a whole ton aboard!

A hundred dollars 'n the Red Box dinghy's
our best offer
It's all we have for trade an' in the coffer
The children're all over the dinghy with delight
while the elders take pity on our plight

A sugar sack stuffed full of product
the fellow produces
Ten thousand dollars back home
this sailor deduces
Calypso sails outa Panama Bay
wearin' big smiles 'n packin' her load 'o hay!

Homeward Bound

Leavin' Punta Mala the mornin' sky is hazy
under Calypso's keel the swell long, low 'n lazy
Land disappears standin' far offshore
how many moons before
she'll touch terra firma once more

Hector

A fresh Pacific breeze sweeps Calypso on her way
she makes a hundred miles the very first day
An' on that first night we learn
'bout this contraption hangin' off her stern

Named for Homer's legendary prince 'n fighter
Hector makes our workload lighter
Steerin' Calypso without food or sleep
regardless the seaway choppy or steep

Daily Routines Evolve

An abundance of fruit hangin' in the rig
skipjack for dinner caught on a jig
All the comforts we're afforded
includin' that sack of produce we've hoarded!

Bumper Crop

Now the afore mentioned sack must be protected
from pryin' eyes 'n remain undetected
A simple plan's devised
usin' a bumper which's oversized

The bumper we pack super tight
an' glue the seam back exactly right
"We'll hang it over the side at our next port
then go to customs an' report!"

Mr. Nimbus

A breathless ocean afternoon heat's oppressive
Billowin' clouds're impressive
The signs cannot be misunderstood
Mr. Nimbus's in the neighborhood!

Tremendous energy accumulates before our eyes
risin' thousands of feet into blue skies
The suspense is particularly frightenin'
'cause there's no thunder 'n lightnin'

Waterspout

From a black knob a tornadic vortex extends
to the ocean's surface the funnel descends
In the face of this danger Calypso stands proud
while a top hat's suckin' ocean into a cloud

Two thousand feet tall this menacin' twister
now we discover it has a sister!
Cumulonimbus produces a storm
where tornadic funnels spawn 'n swarm

Water spouts diggin' trenches in the sea
a harrowin' situation has come to be
Absolutely nothin' can be done
Calypso just sits frozen in the sun

As quickly as Mr. Nimbus appeared
the funnels dissipate 'n disappeared!
These threatenin' twisters havin' receded
Calypso drifts on unimpeded

Chapter 13
April 1981
DOLDRUMS

Northwest Drift

A strong Northwesterly current prevails
still no wind for Calypso's sails
Driftin' along at a comfortable pace
nearly oblivious to the human race

The short wave radio's an exception
to the outside world it's Calypso's connection
Voice of America brings "Mornin' Edition"
"All Things Considered" our evenin' tradition

Aboard Calypso pleasant routines evolve
aroun' navigation 'n fishin' the days revolve
Stars 'n planets captured at first light
breakfast caught on the mornin' bite

A variety of fishin' tools're made
canvas over the mizzen boom for shade
Schools of fish gathern' under the boat
we're discoverin' an idyllic life afloat

A hundred miles
off the Guatemalan coast
caught a nice mackerel for a dinner roast
However that roast never came to be
flipped off the hook 'n back to the sea

Fatlip

The followin' mornin' a curious sight
a Mackerel looks like it'd been in a fight
The fish caught the day before
has a fat lip an' it sure looks sore

Chapter 14
GULF OF TEHUANTEPEC

Doldrums Demise

From the Bay of Campeche
this norther comes a screamin'
Funneled through a mountain pass
this fabled wind's a demon
Taken by surprise at its ferocious arrival
this sea of tranquility now a struggle for survival

Six hundred miles thirty days adrift
a weather change comes very swift
Initial gust hits like a boat wrecker
Calypso just drifted into a Tehuantepecer!

Wind's rippin' at Calypso with a tiger's claw
perfect timin' for Murphy's Law
Tryin' to reef the mizzen as the wind howls
at the masthead the halyard fouls!

To solve this problem there's no doubt
gotta go aloft 'n straighten this mess out
Gustin' sixty seventy knots an' more
this proves to be a most difficult chore

The mizzen mast's not very tall
an' its diameter quite small
Gettin' to the top's in vain
'cause this little mast can't take the strain

Winds howlin' at storm force
Calypso's buckin' like a wild horse
At the top, the mast starts whippin'
it's come down to white knuckles grippin'

Floppin' aroun' top o' the mast
hands let go! They can't hold fast!
Flyin' through the air arms 'n legs flailin'
all splayed out an' silently wailin'

With the boat's extreme motion
damn near flew off into the ocean!
Calypso's thrashin' so wildly
the landin' was rough to put it mildly

Back on deck the solution's revised
a plan to drop the mizzen mast's devised
In calm conditions this task's easy
but at seventy knots it's way too breezy

When all four stays we detach
there ensues a terrific wrestlin' match
A struggle with wind, sail 'n a big wooden stick
tossed by the ocean proves no simple trick

In wind 'n sea Calypso thrashes
onto the deck the mizzen mast crashes
The crew scrambles to make the mast ready
to step again so Calypso'll ride steady

Timin' the lift with the boat's roll's a must
usin' the wind for extra thrust
Up she goes but way too fast!
Back to the deck crashes
the mizzen mast

Ragin' conditions make for a most difficult chore
'cause that mast falls several times more
With perseverance there's success at last
when finally we step the mizzen mast

Squared away the deck and retired below
nuthin to do but ride out the blow
Two more days Calypso's tossed and tumbled
a weary crew sits quietly humbled

Chapter 15
April - May 1981
NORTHEAST TRADEWINDS

Wind drops to fifteen knots on day three
a hundred twenty miles farther out to sea
Raise the mains'l 'n sheet'er tight
let the genny fly 'n set the course right

Blue Pacific swells big 'n bold
a comfortin' gurgle as the breeze takes hold
Tirelessly seekin' the winds' vector
at the helm stands a vigilant Hector

Hitchiker

With Calypso underway
time for breakfast 'n the catch o' the day
Lookin' over the stern a surprisin' sight
There's that mackerel look's like it'd been in a fight!

A tasty fillet's dangled
next to that nose so mangled
But this fish never gives it a look
an' will not touch the baited hook

A tiny tuna swoops in an' gets caught
to this mackerel it matters not
I guess 'ol Fatlip don't hold a grudge
from Calypso's stern he does not budge

The Final Frontier

NPR tells us "Scan the night sky
for a hundred tons of metal hurtlin' by
The Space Shuttle Columbia's up there
in that vast expanse somewhere"

Over a million miles they travel in two days
so much like Calypso in so many ways
In space 'n sea one hears the Sirens' call
Astronauts an' Argonauts adventurers all

Bucking the Trades

The breeze freshens quickly after sunrise
Doldrums are far astern we surmise
Shorten sail as the wind demands
to the north by northwest, Calypso stands

Under jib 'n mizzen Calypso charges ahead
in the crew there's no fear or dread
For challenges ahead eager anticipation
for this moment in time wondrous exhilaration

A train of choppy swells outa' the northeast
ten or twelve feet high at the very least
Slack the sheets, let'er fall off slightly
take these seas a little more lightly

Through this choppy seascape Calypso's slidin'
at her side flyin' fish're glidin'
High above the mast Man-o-War're soarin'
on this glorious trade winds mornin'

A speck of wood on this ocean so vast
a lone Albatross circles the mast
Beatin' to windward the order of the day
a chorus of critters usher Calypso on her way

At the surface shearwaters 'n skuas're skimmin'
In the swells swordfish 'n tuna're finnin'
Calypso's world a livin' collage
On this great ocean with her entourage

Blue Footed Booby Boo Boo

A blue footed booby bird lands on deck
Calypso's crew says "what the heck!"
Thinkin' this poor bird's needin' a rest
never occurred it's lookin' for a nest

A friendly sort big as a turkey
has no interest in tuna fish jerky
An' this Booby's not a lonesome bird
'cause here comes a second an' a third!

All day long boobies're circlin' 'n landin'
on both rails 'n out the bowsprit their standin'
At the top 'o the mast an' on the gaff boom
for another bird there's just no more room

For several days Calypso carries her flock
like a mid-ocean floatin' rock
Buckets of salt water are required
when in guano we are mired

With a bamboo pole they're chased away at dark
not allowin' another bird to park
When mornin' comes no more scrapin' 'n scoopin'
'cause blue footed booby birds ain't a poopin'!

Calypso beats her way north into the ultramarine
the crew returns to the daily routine
Celestial navigation 'n fishin' take precedence
now that our bird friends're no longer in residence

Heavy seas continue to churn
Hector stands tall at Calypso's stern
This mechanical sailor we've mounted
keeps Calypso on course undaunted

Slosh

Day after day Calypso labors to windward
Clipperton Island lies to leeward
Comes a moment in the middle of the night
crew's awakened to the sense somethin's not right

Under the cabin sole there's no mistakin'
the sound of sea water Calypso's takin'
Tear up a floorboard 'n take a peek
sure enough she's opened up a leak

Ten gallons we pump out
plantin' a seed of doubt
"Not our freshwater 'cause it tastes like salt
mebbe its Hector who's at fault?"

Deep Blue

Dive over the side durin' a mornin' lull
find no problem with Calypso's hull
See no damage an' the seams look tight
Calypso's hull appears to be alright

Pumpin' the bilge a daily routine
somethin' the crew had previously seen
Ten gallons a day we're pumpin' now
waters' leakin' from the stern somehow

Loggerhead

To the north by northwest Calypso holds steadfast
forty five days have now passed
A variety of critters entertain the crew
porpoise, whales 'n swordfish to name a few

A loggerhead turtle bumps alongside
Its attraction to Calypso it does not hide
mahi mahi 'n porpoise appear in the swells
behind her stern ol' Fatlip still dwells

Flying Fish

Tasty morsels constantly whizzin' by
the crew gives Flying Fish a try
Gathered several up that got stranded
when on deck they crash landed

Got the estufa fired up 'n fryin'
these little fish that're done flyin'
An' when those critters are sizzlin' hot
the crew could eat them not!

Estufa

Too oily 'n strong these little fish
mahi mahi's our favorite dish!
An' 'bout that estufa by the way
curse that thing several times a day

Smokin' 'n sputterin' when set alight
an eye waterin' throat chokin' fight
An' when the fire gets good 'n hot
yer' cookin' on a fancy smudge pot!

Saltwater 'n soap's a waste of time
all that's doin' is spreadin' the grime
A black 'n gooey sticky gunge
from cabin walls we cannot expunge

Throughout the boat 'n on our clothes
greasy soot from our heads to our toes
A salt water bath or two a day
cannot keep grimy black at bay

Night Sky

The crew sails on to a place unseen
a timeless journey it does seem
Under constellations we so rely
Calypso's in harmony with sea 'n sky

Draped in a blanket of tiny lights
Arcturus, Spica 'n the moon offer accurate sights
With these friends in the vast expanse
Calypso's position is not left to chance
Twelve hundred miles west of San Francisco
'bout the same distance east of Hilo
There's a patch of ocean where Calypso will be tackin'
an' to the Strait of Juan de Fuca she'll begin trackin'

Inventory

Closin' in on sixty days at this endeavor
takin' stock of water 'n stores not a pleasure
Of the current situation the crew is not oblivious
cause' the shortage of fresh water is quite obvious

Beans, rice 'n flour there's plenty
eggs're gettin' low, just twenty
It's quite amazin' in this tropical heat
the eggs're still okay to eat

Nearin' two months without rain
from soakin' beans in fresh water we abstain
Rationin' this precious commodity
to reduce consumption
fifty days remainin's our assumption

Twelve hundred miles sixty days at sea
Strait of Juan de Fuca no longer a possibility
Averagin' forty miles a day the crew had to balk
'cause that's 'bout as fast as we could just walk

"Only five hundred miles to 'ol Mexico
we can run downwind for Acapulco!
Four or five days easy sailin'
we'll stop the leak an' won't be bailin'

Course Change

Sloshin' bilge, shortages 'n slow speed
for Calypso's crew its decision time indeed
"Crossin' the Great Ocean's best" the I Ching reports
"Hawaii's thirty seven hundred miles west!"
The navigator retorts

Chapter 16
May - June 1981
DOWNWIND TO HAWAII

Douse the mizzen 'n slack the mainsheet
helm to port 'n quit this upwind beat
Out to starboard the genny flies
under pearly white clouds
scuddin' 'cross blue skies

Slidin' down twelve footers wind at her back
for Hawaii Calypso's on the right tack
Sails're set runnin' wing 'n wing
if only this little boat could sing!

Calypso has an easy motion
rollin' with the Pacific Ocean
Stars floatin' past the hatch at night
this run for the Islands feelin' just right

Navigation's way more fun
takin' sights of stars, moon 'n sun
Lines of position showin' headway
Calypso's makin' a hundred miles a day!

Seaborne Circus

Continuin' on with her entourage
a thousand Dolphins leapin' n' twirlin' is no mirage
Sharks join in a frenzied feast
on the remains of some poor hapless beast

Swordfish circle 'n whack their prey
mahi mahi's the catch o' the day
An' speakin' of fish on the bite
good 'ol Fatlip's still hangin' tight!

Seventy three days out
the crew has no doubt
Life at sea with all the critters around
is truly a life of freedom unbound

Pumping Seawater

Pumpin' day 'n night now the chore
cause' Calypso's leakin' more 'n more
A pesky leak increasin' as we make our way
Calypso's takin' eighty gallons a day!

Over the shortwave radio
world news continues to flow
The Pope 'n President've both been shot
but to the crew of Calypso it matters not'

Cause we're at sea in a sinkin' boat
no idea how long we'll stay afloat
Popes 'n Presidents're not our concern
Calypso's got water pourin' in from the stern!

Playin' backgammon 'n throwin' dice
makin' tortillas, beans 'n rice
Days are all kinda serene
even sinkin' seems routine

Bumper Crop

The supply's low an' there's a need to replenish
that produce for which the crew has a fetish
A serrated knife leaves the bumper agape
so it's patched up with glue 'n duct tape!

Fatlip Chocks One Up

Right after the routine mornin' sight
always taken at the crack of first light
Lean over the stern check on that fish
that narrowly avoided our supper dish

An' 'ol Fatlip's always there
lookin' up with that mournful stare
Never gives the bait a second look
ever since he flipped off that hook

Every time a fish gets caught
for scraps he's johnny on the spot
Thousands of miles 'ol Fatlip has swum
this hardy little mackerel's not so dumb!

Fresh Water 'n Sun Rot

For a deluge the crew's been a wishin'
a tropical downpour's the only thing missin'
Freshwater showers'd make life even better
'cause salt water 'n sun's turnin' soft skin to leather

The mainsail's cause for concern
as that tropical sun continues to burn
Haul it in an' make repairs
durin' early morning's lighter airs

Patchin's hard work 'n takes some time
then hoist the main 'n get 'er back on line
Calypso goes chargin' ahead, sailin' full tilt
lookin' like Cosmic Chris an' his patchwork quilt!

Racin' along at breakneck speed
exhilaratin' ridin' our trusty steed
Seven hundred miles covered in a week
a thousand gallons pumped
stayin' ahead o' the leak!

Makin' our way to the twentieth parallel
eighty days at sea 'n all's well
Food 'n water still holdin' out
plenty of fish swimmin' about

Trades pump up considerably in the afternoon
fillin' Calypso's genny like a big white balloon
Guidin' her through the night is Hector
tirelessly trackin' the trade wind's vector

Sinking

Still stayin' ahead of the water comin' in
determined not to let it win
But what if the pump should give out
an' the crew can no longer hold out?

"There's a ton of ballast in the bottom of the boat
we'll just toss it all overboard an' still float!
The idea's really not daft
after all, Kon Tiki was just a raft!"

With that comfortin' thought Calypso sails along
an' with the daily routines, the crew carry on
Closin' in on a thousand miles to their destination
they tend their pump without hesitation

The daytime sky's filled with aids to navigation
thousands of people flyin' to the Islands on vacation
Contrails from all the major cities are convergin'
to a point over the horizon
where Hawaii will be emergin'

The AM radio's comin' in handy
as a direction finder it's a dandy
Pointin' out stations on Hawaii 'n California
correspondin' what the stars
sun 'n moon're tellin' ya

Closing in

A wonderful sail we really don't want to quit
"We'll put on food 'n water 'n refit
stop the leakin' 'n patch the sails
then follow the trade winds
an' the Humpback Whales!"

Closin' in on these Islands of the Pacific
the Ocean sends a message humorous yet specific
Got slapped in the face by a fish leapin'
an' 'leavin' this sailor thankfully weepin'

A school of mahi mahi iridescent 'n bright
appear in a wave bathed in mornin' light
Eye to eye with these beautiful fish
one could hear the Oceans' wish

The message to the crew's loud 'n clear
these wonderful creatures have been very dear
A debt of gratitude there will always be
for these most magnificent mahi mahi

So now beans 'n rice the mainstay
an' a small tuna or two a day
An' still waitin' for scraps with that soulful stare
good 'ol Fatlip's still there

The Leak

That 'ol bronze pump ya work by hand
the crew's pumpin' to beat the band
Throughout each night 'n all day long
somethin' down below's gone way wrong

Slosh...slosh...slosh...KERSPLOSH!
slosh...slosh...slosh...KERSPLOSH!
Calypsos' bilge alarm's the motion
of a rhythmic rollin' heavin' ocean

As Calypso approaches her destination
the leak's still cause for consternation
These gallons we're pumpin' we no longer count
the crew only knows it's a huge amount

Eyes're now scannin' the horizon '
cause soon there'll be land arisin'
Pumpin' seawater we'll do no more
we'll have showers, pizza 'n beer galore!

Crossin' the hundred fiftieth meridian today
more 'n more contrails're pointin' our way
Sailin' the twenty north latitude line
a followin' sea 'n makin' great time

Day ninety-three at first light
get up 'n take the mornin' sight
Throw 'ol Fatlip a breakfast snack
sit in the cockpit 'n kick back

Calypso's risin' 'n fallin' in a heavy seaway
a ten foot swell runnin' today
From top of one of these rollin' blue hills
a sight on the horizon gives the crew chills

Climbin' the riggin' to get a better view
smiles're glowin' on Calypso 'n crew
The unmistakable sight of land poppin' up 'n down
gettin' intermittent glimpses of Mauna Kea's crown

Chapter 17
1981
HILO HAWAII

The mountain's presence now dominates
that small nob in the distance captivates
Calypso's sailin' as if possessed
the crew's sailin' as if obsessed

We discover where land 'n sea meet
the whole experience bittersweet
Caught in conflict with the notion
of leavin' this wondrous Pacific Ocean

Coastline Struggle

Two days more the mountain's standin' tall
Calypso will soon arrive at her port 'o call
After ninety-six days we'll make our way
into the arms of Hilo Bay

Nearin' our goal winds get fluky
the current's strong 'n situation spooky
Cause' without headway there's a danger here
from the Island chain Calypso will be swept clear

Throughout the night
Calypso 'n crew endure this fright
Aware of this precarious pinch
Calypso's scratchin' 'n clawin' for every inch

Tackin' back 'n forth close by the shoreline
Calypso catches a counter current in the nick of time
Mid-afternoon of her ninety seventh day
she's sailin' into Hilo Bay

Fatlip's Farewell

Up ahead a color change causes concern
the crew scrambles to look over the stern
To say goodbye to 'ol Fatlip, our friend the fish
who never wound up on the supper dish

Tossin' scraps to 'ol Fatlip always brought smiles
this little mackerel swimmin' thousands of miles
Strainin' to get the very last look
at our little friend who outsmarted the hook

Hilo Bay

In Hilo bay the wind quits
givin' the crew the fits
Wonderin' "can this really be?"
Calypso's driftin' back out to sea!

Appears Mauna Kea's offerin' Calypso a gift
the entrance buoy's in the path of her drift
A favorable puff of wind an' on the first try
gotta line round that buoy as we're floatin' by

Hangin' off this giant red anchor for survival
a pitiful scene, our momentous arrival
However it gives the crew time to make a plan
of what to do 'bout Mr. Customs man!

Bumper Business

Dug the bumper from outa the bow
ponderin' "whadda we do now?
We can set the thing afloat
or hang it over the side of the boat?!"

When we're tyin' up to the dock
that 'ol bumper's gotta take up the shock
The pressure's a heavy load
that duct taped' bumper 's gonna explode!

Good Samaritan

A Good Samaritan sails in from the west coast
Calypso gets a tow line an' invited to a pig roast!
A crowd's gatherin' 'n helpin' out
"That's the missin' boat!"
a Coast Guardsman shouts out

The Coastguard's in a dither
up 'n down the dock runnin' hither tither
This alert young fella's in the know
Calypso'd been reported missin' two months ago!

Mr. Customs Man

Mr. Customs man arrives impeccably dressed
lookin' down at Calypso visibly unimpressed
Gingerly he steps aboard our floatin' hovel
grime so thick he shoulda' brung a shovel!

Preoccupied with stayin' clean
he's gingerly surveyin' this grungy scene
Makin' a couple notes in his book
never givin' that 'ol bumper a second look!

Potluck

Steppin' off the dock onto dry land
the crowd gives the crew a big hand
Calypso's arrival's cause for celebration
an' the barbecue's fired up for the occasion!

The folks're full of questions now
of what where when 'n how?
The crew explain the journey as best they could
an' these world sailors 'n locals understood

Tables're piled high with food, beer 'n wine
these folks know how to have a good time
Pizza 'n poke 'n cake 'n ice cream
everthin' a sailor could dream!

Burgers 'n dogs sizzlin' on the grill
we're gonna eat our fill!
Pilin' a plate high with goodies
'n grabbin' a glass of wine
Calypso's crew sits down to dine

A few small bites into this feast we take
start feelin' the 'ol belly ache
What at first we thought a real treat
all this food we cannot eat!

When out at sea we thought we'd eat like hogs
now we're tossin' burgers to the dogs!
When before we thought we were payin' a price
now we're missin' our raw fish, beans 'n rice!

Chapter 18
June - August 1981
BEACHED

Naval Shipworms

First order of business when the tide goes out
find what this miserable leak's all about
The crew examines her hull all around
at first glance she appears sound

Lookin' inside the boat again
"Yup! The waters' still pourin' in!
No visible damage anywhere
but there's water comin' in everywhere!?"

Calypso's boot stripe's painted blue
an' here's where Pat finds a clue
With close observation she becomes wary
"What're these tiny little holes?" is her query

Proddin' 'n pokin' prove our worst fears true
when the knife just pushes right on through
The bootstripe served as an open hatch
where parasites could happily attach

'Haulout

Sail 'round to the public park on the risin' tide
where a crane shows up 'n takes Calypso for a ride
On terra firma the crew stands with a solemn stare
at their sweet little Calypso way up in the air

A shady spot's found to park it
right by "Suisan Fish Market"
Sam Kumukahi takes the crew under his wing
An' his gang of friends who love to drink beer 'n sing!

Naval shipworms had been makin' tunnels
from Calypso's keel to her gunnels
Bi-valves with a shell on their head
this is the critter wooden boats dread

With our boat worms're havin' a great time
'cause they're dinin' on sweet
New England white pine
Our tough little vessel in 'n outa so many jams
an' now poor Calypso's got the clams

Surrounded by this Aloha atmosphere
The crew jumps into high gear
With a vengeance that's feelin' real good
rippin' 'n tearin' worm eaten wood

Planks so thin the impression they give
Calypso's become a seawater sieve
Teredos have kept the crew pumpin'
now their gettin' a real good thumpin'!

Repair and Refit

Cuttin' out bad wood doesn't take long
fourteen planks completely gone
Saws 'n planes, chisels 'n drills donated
nails, screws 'n goopucky preferences debated

Pick up the lines with a spile
mahogany boards waitin' in a pile
Makin' patterns 'n cuttin' out planks
to Sam 'n his gang we owe so many thanks!

Work slows some to a relaxin' pace
'cause in Hawaii life isn't a race
But storm winds of September will soon prevail
an' for the North Pacific Calypso must sail

The corkin' hammer rings nearin' works' end
returnin' to sea's right 'round the bend
Drivin' oakum 'n cotton into her seams
paintin' the bottom of this boat of our dreams

The big day soon arrives
time for Calypso' n crew to say their goodbyes
Friends gather in the Aloha Way
Calypso sails quietly outa' Hilo Bay

Chapter 19
August 1981
NORTH PACIFIC OCEAN

Returnin' to life at sea 'n familiar routines
it's that thing of storybooks 'n daydreams
Not pumpin' the bilge its dry's a bone
chargin' over blue seas 'n headin' home!

Pickin' up the trades roundin' the headland
spirits soarin' 'n the crew's feelin' grand
But for Calypso somethins' missin'
it's for 'ol Fatlip she's a wishin'

Her tag along sidekick for so many miles
followin' Calypso through so many trials
Hopin' her best friend's found a new home
an' wonderin' if 'ol Fatlip still has an urge to roam

Due North

Sailin' along Hawaii's windward side
Calypsos' havin' a great ride
A beam reach in fine weather
all dried out 'n light as a feather

More'n fifteen degrees north latitude gained
Polaris risin' higher as if unchained
A thousand miles an' the trades're holdin' steady
ten days out 'n the crew's rough 'n ready

Gotta mention it ain't flowin' like a creek
but Calypso's opened up a new leak
Maybe the transom's got Teredos
them miserable microscopic torpedoes!

Weather Change

Wakin' to a change in the weather
tossin' boat says it ain't changin' for the better
Wind's outa the northwest today
deep blue seas now battleship grey

This cold wind it's bitin'
a rough ocean Calypso's fightin'
Increasin' now gale force blowin'
two hours more 'n the storm's still growin'

Storm Riders

Hove to under reefed mizzen
hurricane force 'n seas have risen
Every breakin' wave Calypso catches
water blows through portholes 'n hatches

The Great Wave

Calypso's bein' tumbled 'n trashed
crew's hunkered below soakin' cold 'n thrashed
In the middle of the night wake to a scare
floatin' off the bunk weightless in midair

While Calypso's free fallin' in space
the minds's thinkin' "we're gonna leave no trace!"
A fifty or hundred foot wave the truth be told
"when we hit the trough she's gonna explode!"

"Gonna be the end of this madness!"
as Calypso plummets through the blackness
When back into the ocean she crashes
onto the cabin sole this flyin' sailor splashes!

Now this soakin' wet mattress feels real good
protected by this bundle of nails, screws 'n wood
Thinkin' "this is gonna be one to remember
this Equinox storm of mid-September"

Three days more weather stays foul
wind simply will not cease to howl
A relentless march of greybeard waves
reminders of Calypso's many close shaves

On this fine mornin' of the sixth day
The greybeards have finally gone away
Wind's twenty knots outa the northwest
Calypso survived her North Pacific test

Murphy

Emergin' from our sea soaked abode
the crew's back into sailin' mode
Fresh winds fillin' the genny 'n main
sun's shinin' 'n there ain't no rain

Shakin' out the reef 'n raisin' the mizzen sail
it's the mizzen halyards' turn to fail
Gotta repair it before the next storms arrival
'cause its Calypso's rig for heavy weather survival

Once before the mizzen was scaled
an' that attempt miserably failed
But pullin' the mast down was a difficult chore
so it's decided to climb the mizzen mast once more

Timin' moves with the boat's roll
made it the top of this skinny pole
While gripin' stays with white knuckles
the mizzen mast whips snaps 'n buckles!

The stays keep the mizzen mast standin'
on deck this sailor makes a hard landin'
Got the mast lashed 'n sistered
with hands all bleedin' 'n blistered

Bringin' the mizzen back on line
we accomplish in the nick of time
Only a few hours sailin' toward our goal
the crew can see it's a sucker hole!

Batten Down the Hatches

With reefed mizzen 'n helm lashed tight
Calypso's readied for the next fight
Skies darken 'n grey seas return
there's dirty weather brewin' off her stern

Steadily the ocean lump's beginin' to grow
cold northwest wind startin' to blow
In black clouds Calypso's soon cloaked
down below bunks're cold 'n soaked

It's a wonder how Calypso behaves
bouncin' 'round in these giant waves
White capped crests constantly smackin' her hull
the crew patiently waits for the next lull

The crew hunkers down three days more
no chance to dry out 'n gettin' bedsore
Sun greets the mornin' on the fourth day
set full sail 'n get Calypso underway

One thing for sure it's goin' our way
this nasty weather's headed to Neah Bay
Weather's gearin' up for the season's change
the Strait of Juan de Fuca's straight downrange

Psychedelic Ocean

In the ways she finds to tantalize
the ocean never ceases to surprise
This blue Pacific mornin's no exception
when she toys with the crew's visual perception

Light bathes the sea turnin' it blue
revealin' a spectacle to the crew
Far as the eye can see on every swell
she casts her magical spell

Bedecked, bedazzled bejeweled 'n ballooned
with colorful glass fishin' floats she's festooned
As many as practical the crew collected
these ocean gifts so unexpected

An amazin' sail which has come to be
a magic carpet ride on this slow rollin' sea
Risin' sun sets glass floats afire
psychedelic sailin' through the North Pacific Gyre

Gotta sun sight right at noon
got another on the moon
Calypso's averaged seventy-five miles a day
just eight hundred miles to Neah Bay

Calypso's world's surreal for three days
while bathin' in a bright suns' rays
Nights're crystal clear 'n crisp
at the horizons' edge a low lying mist

The sea's rise is almost imperceptible
then grow quickly to a size quite respectable
The shift in the wind's very slight
an' it still carries that cold northern bite

Neptune's Rage

Barometer's fallin' like a stone
wind's chillin' the crew to the bone
Top of the waves white caps appear
in the crew of Calypso this raises no fear

After two years sailin' the crew has learned
Calypso's a tough little boat
an' our respect she's earned
The crew hops to an' gets the deck squared away
gonna be driftin' on a reefed mizzen today

Risin' seas whisper "more wind's a comin' "
the riggin' chimes in an' starts a hummin'
Top 'o the waves wind stings the eyes
at the troughs bottom the cold wind dies

A low grey cloud appears
the wind cranks up as if changin' gears
The anvil arrives with its leadin' edge
an' it's like gettin' hit with Neptune's sledge

The initial blow lays Calypso on her side
sendin' her slidin' down the waves' backside
The blast is hurricane force
an' it's blowin' Calypso right on course

The mizzen sail sets her bow to weather
Calypso floats on this ocean light as a feather
The anvil quickly passes by
an' like a thief steals the blue sky

One after another marchin' in succession
the storms of September in a grand procession
On leavin' Hilo the crew never had the notion
they'd be sailin' backwards 'cross the ocean

Closing In

Cloud covered days 'n dark stormy nights
two weeks waitin' for those precious star sights
Not takin' navigation by chance
sailin' by compass 'n seat of the pants

At long last a break in the weather
a change in this pattern's for the better
Sights're taken right at dawn
then lines of position carefully drawn

Thirty-five hundred miles outa' Hilo
Storm petrels n' Shearwaters're greetin' Calypso
A mere two hundred miles to the West Coast
Of a tough Equinox crossin' Calypso can boast

Chapter 20
October 1981
A JOURNEY'S END

Continental Shelf

Where ocean turns from blue to green
the Continental Shelf is clearly seen
Gulls're now circlin' 'n swoopin' nearby
to the North Pacific Ocean we'll soon say goodbye

Fog Bound

Thick mornin' fog on day thirty-seven
starts breakin' up just after eleven
Olympic mountains're lookin' grand
curtain's liftin' on an evergreen land

Terra firma visible to the north 'n south
the Strait of Juan de Fuca's gapin' mouth
Glassy calm 'n ebbin' this afternoon
the tide'll be turnin' 'n floodin' soon

Sun burns last of the fog away
tide turns at the end of the day
The crew can hear the current's gurglin' whoosh
when Calypso goes driftin' close by Tatoosh

Goin' with the flow on this windless drift
this flood tide's nature's gift
A panorama of lights replace the daylight
when Calypso goes driftin' into the night

Nightfall

A myriad of lights nearly overwhelm
the lookout steadfast at the helm
Shippin' lanes're real busy
so much traffic the crew's gettin' dizzy

Tugs 'n barges 'n ships all about
great difficulty sortin' all the lights out
Bright lights ashore add to the confusion
of what's real 'n what's an illusion

Logship

Two lights appear of a ship previously unseen
most definitely they're red 'n green
At first just a twinklin', a couple minutes later
Pat's yellin' "It's a freighter!"

The moment's shattered with her shout
"Get life preservers 'n flashlights out!"
Driftin' in a dead calm Calypso has no recourse
'cause she's on a deadly collision course!

Middle of the night her big engines pound
hearts are racin' at the sound
Black steel towerin' in the night
this homecomin's an absolute fright

Freighter's bearin' down, crew's standin' transfixed
on the sails flashlights are fixed
After thousands of miles 'n so many trials
we're gonna end our trip
on the bow of this big 'ol ship!

The crew's hangin' onto the mast ready to jump
the instant Calypso takes that first big bump
Time slows to a crawl as the last moments passed
starin' at that bow where Calypso will be dashed

Ever so slight the lights give a shudder
when the helmsman hits hard-over
on the ship's rudder
Those red n' green lights go cockeyed
as that ship heels over on her starboard side
Musta' rolled the crew right outa their beds
an' sent the capt'n runnin' for his meds!

In the black of night the world's surreal
when the bow wake takes Calypso by her keel
A sickenin' surge from under her port side
then that wave just tosses Calypso aside

Thanks to the helmsman's quick thinkin'
Calypso's not dashed to pieces 'n sinkin'!
The ship leaves Calypso floppin' in her wake
not a scratch on her does it make
The crew held on 'n didn't jump ship
that'd been a lousy end to a pretty good trip!

Saturday October 10, 1981

Calypso's sails fill with an early mornin' breeze
into Neah Bay she tacks with ease
After thousands of miles 'n two years
the crew's at anchor sharin' laughs 'n tears

Afterthought

Oh! That little business venture?
Just another misadventure!
Thought we'd fill the coffers to the top
With our Panamanian bumper crop

Months at sea did not serve the contraband well
Makin' seaweed impossible to sell
When all was said 'n done in PT 'n Hilo
Calypso never peddled a single kilo!

GLOSSARY

Aft / Abaft	Stern- Toward / from
Bight	secures a line / a small cove
Block	Pulley
Boom	Carries foot (bottom) of sail
Bow	Front of boat
Bread	Money
Cleat(s)	Strong point for making lines off
Cuke(s)	Sea cucumber (Bivalve)
Dinghy	Sailboat tender (Rinky Dink)
Draft	Depth of water to bottom of keel
Ebb(ing)	Tide going out (receding)
Fathom(s)	One fathom=6 feet water depth
Fatlip	A mackerel befriended swam 5000 mi.
Flood(ing)	Tide coming in (rising)
Gaff rig / boom	Boom carried aloft for attaching sails
Garboard	Structural plank / joint at top of keel
Halyard(s)	Line(s) that raise & lower sails
Hector	A self-steering mechanical contraption
Helm	Steering wheel
Hook (pick)	Anchor
I-Ching	Chinese navigation tool
"In Irons"	Boat holds bow into wind
Keel	Structural "spine" of the boat
Ketch	Two masted sailboat (main & mizzen)
Knot(s)	Speed
Lee (leeward)	Downwind side of boat
Mile	Nautical mile (6000 ft.)
Mizzen	Smaller mast aft of the mainmast
Port	Left (Starboard=Right)
Sheet(s)	Lines control sails port & starboard
Skiff	Small workboat

Color (print)
Ballad of Calypso, Rhyme of the Modern Mariner
ISBN 978-0-5783505-4-7

B&W (print)
Calypso, Rhyme of the Modern Mariner
ISBN 978-0-5789121-4-1

EPUB (color)
Ballad of Calypso, Rhyme of the Modern Mariner
ISBN 978-0-5789121-5-8

COMPANION TO CALYPSO

B&W (print)
ISBN 979-8-218-36093-1

EPUB (B&W)
ISBN 979-8-218-35969-0

www.ingramcontent.com/pod-product-compliance
Lightning Source LLC
Chambersburg PA
CBHW051233160726
47994CB00002B/866